"Teach the children so that it will not be necessary to teach the adults."
—President Abraham Lincoln

"I never teach my pupils; I only attempt to provide the conditions in which they can learn."
—Albert Einstein

"The function of education is to teach one to think intensively and to think critically... Intelligence plus character - that is the goal of true education."
—Martin Luther King, Jr.

"I have come to believe that a great teacher is a great artist and that there are as few as there are any other great artists. Teaching might even be the greatest of the arts since the medium is the human mind and spirit."
—John Steinbeck

"The greatest sign of success for a teacher...is to be able to say, 'The children are now working as if I did not exist.'"
—Maria Montessori

"Give a man a fish and you feed him for a day. Teach a man to fish and you feed him for a lifetime."
—Proverb

Other books in the **When I Grow Up I Want To Be...** children's book series by Wigu Publishing:

When I Grow Up I Want To Be... in the U.S. Army!
When I Grow Up I Want To Be... Firefighter!
When I Grow Up I Want To Be... in the U.S. Navy!
When I Grow Up I Want To Be... a Veterinarian!
When I Grow Up I Want To Be... a Nurse!

Look for these titles in the **When I Grow Up I Want To Be...** children's book series soon:

When I Grow Up I Want To Be... a Good Person!
When I Grow Up I Want To Be... a World Traveler!
When I Grow Up I Want To Be... a Race Car Driver!
When I Grow Up I Want To Be... a Police Officer!
When I Grow Up I Want To Be... Green!
When I Grow Up I Want To Be... a Rock Star!
When I Grow Up I Want To Be... in the U.S. Air Force!

Cuando Crezca Quiero Ser... coming soon!

Please visit www.whenigrowupbooks.com for more information.
Please like us at www.facebook.com/whenigrowupbooksbywigu.

When I Grow Up I Want To Be...®
a Teacher!

Carlee Learns a Surprising Lesson!

Wigu Publishing | Sun Valley, ID

Copyright © 2013 by Wigu Publishing, LLC

Illustrations copyright © 2013 by Wigu Publishing, LLC

All rights reserved. No part of this publication may be reproduced, distributed, or transmitted in any form or by any means, including photocopying, recording, or other electronic or mechanical methods, without the prior written permission of the publisher, except in the case of brief quotations embodied in critical reviews and certain other noncommercial uses permitted by copyright law. For permission requests, please write to the publisher at the address below.

Library of Congress Control Number: 2013914095

ISBN 978-1-939973-08-5

When I Grow Up I Want To Be... is a registered trademark of Wigu Publishing, LLC. The word Wigu and the Wigu logo are registered trademarks of Wigu Publishing, LLC. The words When I Grow Up... and Cuando Crezca Quiero Ser... are trademarks and/or registered trademarks of Wigu Publishing, LLC.

Wigu Publishing is a collaboration among talented and creative individuals working together to publish informative and fun books for our children. Our titles serve to introduce children to the people in their communities who serve others through their vocations. Wigu's books are unique in that they help our children to visualize the abundant opportunities that exist for them to be successful and to make a difference. Our goal is to inspire the great leaders and thinkers of tomorrow.

First edition, paperback, 2013

10 9 8 7 6 5 4 3 2 1

Quantity sales: Special discounts are available on quantity purchases by corporations, associations, promotional organizations, and others. For details, please contact the publisher at

Wigu Publishing

P.O. Box 1800

Sun Valley, ID 83353

inquiries@wigupublishing.com

Please visit our website at www.whenigrowupbooks.com for more information.

Proudly printed and bound in the United States of America.

This book is dedicated to all of you who grew up to be teachers and to all of you who will.

Carlee is a girl who discovers that not everything you learn in school is found in textbooks. One of Carlee's most important lessons is the one she learns about herself.

Carlee always wanted to be a teacher and she always loved starting a new school year.

Not anymore.

Today is the first day of school and the worst day of my life, and it's all my mother's fault! Carlee fretted over breakfast.

My mother just got a new job. She is a new teacher at my school, and she is even teaching in my grade level.

This is not like kindergarten. Back then, I liked it when Mom helped in class. Now, she is just going to embarrass me, Carlee worried as she boarded the school bus.

Last year, Carlee liked it when her mom drove her to school. This year, she was glad to be riding the bus. She did not want to be seen arriving at school with her mother, the teacher!

There's Mary Katherine. She's probably in my mom's class.

"Hey, Carlee. Guess what?" said Mary Katherine.

I knew it. She's going to tease me in front of everyone on the bus. Why didn't I walk to school?

Carlee tried to look away, but it only made Mary Katherine talk even louder.

Then Mary Katherine said, "We have the same backpack."

Carlee sighed. She put on her headphones and didn't say anything for the rest of the ride to school.

As the bus rolled on its way, Carlee wondered, *What if everyone thinks my mom is lame? What if my mother gives out bad grades? No one will invite me to play. No one will come to my birthday party. No one at school will ever talk to me again because my mom is the teacher. And I bet my teacher will tell my mom every little mistake I make.*

Carlee walked into school with her head down.

She asked herself, *Why couldn't my mom be something else? Like a firefighter. Or a veterinarian. Why can't she teach someplace else? Like France. She says she likes Paris!*

When I grow up, I am going to be anything but a teacher.

The school bell rang and Carlee headed directly to her classroom with her head tucked even farther down. She wanted to be invisible.

Carlee tried to cheer up as she sat in her assigned seat. She looked at her new teacher and thought, *I bet her kids don't go to school here. I bet they get to go to some other school far away.*

"Good morning, class. My name is Mrs. Frank, and I am your teacher this year."

The class responded, "Good morning, Mrs. Frank."

Mrs. Frank took roll. Carlee's friend Hannah was absent. Carlee wondered where she was.

After roll call Mrs. Frank talked about the classroom rules. Mostly they were the same each year. Carlee could imagine her mother saying the same things in the classroom next door and all the kids giggling and whispering about her.

I'm never going to be a teacher like my mother, thought Carlee.

Then Mrs. Frank passed out new textbooks.

"This year we are going to learn a lot of new things," said Mrs. Frank. "Our social studies textbook will include history and geography. We are going to start with geography.

"Does anyone want to tell the class why geography is important?" asked Mrs. Frank.

Carlee liked geography. She could name all seven continents in order of size.

At that moment, Carlee heard the classroom door slowly open with a squeak.

Oh no! Maybe it's Mom stopping by to say hello! Carlee put her head down on the desk and covered her eyes with her hands.

She heard Mrs. Frank say, "Please join us!"

Carlee peeked through the little cracks between her fingers.

It was not her mom but her friend Hannah, late for class on the first day of school! She was always late. *I bet she's glad her mom is not a teacher!*

"We are discussing geography, Hannah. Please find your seat," continued Mrs. Frank. "Geography is important because we must know where we are in the world. We must understand the countries and cultures all around us. Geography helps us map out our world."

Carlee sighed. *Well, I'll never teach geography, but I will travel the world someday. Maybe I'll use geography to go someplace else, do something else, be anything else! I could be an archeologist, an explorer, or an airline pilot—anything but a teacher.*

Marco Polo (ca. 1254–1324) was an Italian merchant and explorer from Venice. Polo traveled with his father and uncle through Asia, which was an unknown part of the world for most Europeans at that time. He spent 24 years exploring the Asian continent. Marco Polo's books about his travels helped people learn about Asia. He inspired future explorers, including Christopher Columbus.

Christopher Columbus (1451–1506) was an Italian explorer who sailed under the flag of Spain. In 1492, he set out to find a new route to the East Indies. These Asian islands were famous for their riches and spices, but the traditional route was dangerous. Columbus made four voyages. He insisted he had found the famous islands. He called the native people "indios," which is Spanish for "Indians." However, what he had really found was the New World, what would later become America.

The Lewis and Clark Expedition, begun in 1804, was the first American expedition to explore and map out the new western part of the United States. President Thomas Jefferson directed Captain Meriwether Lewis and Second Lieutenant William Clark to lead a group of volunteers from the U.S. Army. Their team set out from St. Louis, Missouri, and traveled westward to the Pacific Coast. This trek paved the way for the westward growth of the United States.

"We will learn a lot more history this year, too," said Mrs. Frank. "History is important because it helps us understand how we got here.

The school bus brought me to school. That's how I got here, Carlee thought. *But that's probably not what Mrs. Frank means.*

"We will learn about famous people and famous events. But what I want you to think about in our history units is how some people made good decisions and others made bad ones."

Like my mom being a teacher at my school, thought Carlee.

"And how we can all learn from the choices people have made, both right and wrong."

I choose not to be a teacher when I grow up, thought Carlee. *But I guess there are lots of ways to be famous and make history. Maybe I'll be an astronaut or a great leader!*

Or president of the United States!

Martin Luther King, Jr. (1929–1968) was born Michael King. His father changed his name to honor the German church reformer Martin Luther. King was a Baptist minister who became a leader in the African-American Civil Rights Movement. King fought for equal rights for African Americans by organizing nonviolent protests, including the famous March on Washington, where he delivered his "I Have a Dream" speech. Because of his efforts, King was awarded the Nobel Peace Prize in 1964. After his tragic murder in 1968, King was awarded the Presidential Medal of Freedom and the Congressional Gold Medal.

On July 21, 1969, an American astronaut, **Neil Armstrong** (1930–2012), became the first man to walk on the moon. He was part of a three-man crew on the Apollo 11 flight. Armstrong studied and trained for many years, first as a Navy pilot and then as an astronaut. After his famous trip to the moon, Armstrong became a teacher at the University of Cincinnati. Do you think he brought moon rocks to show his class?

Carlee and her classmates put away their new social studies books and organized their desks. Afterward, Mrs. Frank said it was library time. She told the class to line up in a neat row and quietly walk down the hall to the library.

Carlee remembered Ms. Fischer, the librarian, from last year. Carlee got to be the class library assistant once a week. She got to help Ms. Fischer put books away in the right places. Carlee helped younger kids find books. Ava helped, too. It was fun.

"Welcome back, Carlee!" Ms. Fischer said. "Are you going to be one of my helpers again this year?"

"Sure!" Carlee said.

Then Ms. Fischer went and ruined it all when she said in front of the whole class, "Carlee, I understand your mother is a new teacher here. That must be exciting."

It seemed as if the whole world stopped, and every kid stared right at Carlee. She wished she could shrink herself small enough to hide in one of the books.

Carlee closed her eyes and shuddered. *I am not going to be a teacher, and now I'm not going to be a librarian, either, which is almost like a teacher, even though it was fun being a library helper.*

Benjamin Franklin was born on January 17, 1706, in Boston, Massachusetts. Most kids know Ben Franklin as one of America's Founding Fathers and as a brilliant inventor and statesman. But did you know Franklin is also famous for founding America's first lending library in 1731? Franklin's Library Company of Philadelphia was the forerunner of today's free public libraries. For a brief period, Franklin even served as the company's librarian!

"Tell me and I forget, teach me and I may remember, involve me and I learn."
—Benjamin Franklin

Mrs. Frank thanked the librarian and then told the class, "We are scheduled for physical education three days per week this year, and we are lucky to have PE on our very first day back."

Carlee usually liked PE, even though Mr. Williams, the PE teacher, had greasy hair and talked too loud. He was strict sometimes, too. Her friend Noah said Mr. Williams was like an Army drill sergeant. The class went outside. Mr. Williams was waiting for them.

"Welcome to physical education!" boomed Mr. Williams.

"Does anyone know why we do PE?" he asked in his loud voice.

"Because it's fun?" replied David.

"Right! And?"

"Because they make us," said Tommy. The class laughed. Mr. Williams did not.

Carlee hoped Mr. Williams was not going to say, "There is no 'I' in the word 'team.'" He said that a thousand times a year.

"In PE we learn teamwork! There is no 'I' in the word 'team'!" shouted Mr. Williams.

Carlee rolled her eyes. *I'll never be a PE teacher for sure. But if I get really good at sports I can do something else, something that won't embarrass my kids. Being an Olympic swimmer or a volleyball star or a soccer champion—now that would be cool!*

Back in the classroom, it was time for art. Mrs. Frank said there would be one music class and one art class each week.

"Understanding fine arts, like music and painting, is important because developing your creativity helps you learn new ways to think about things and look at problems," said Mrs. Frank.

It won't help my problem, thought Carlee. *My mom will still be a teacher.*

Carlee thought of all the artsy things she could do besides teaching, like being a rock star or an actor. *Or maybe a video game designer!* she thought.

I could even be a famous artist!

Leonardo da Vinci (1452–1519) was an Italian Renaissance painter, sculptor, architect, musician, mathematician, engineer, inventor, anatomist, geologist, cartographer, botanist, and writer. His painting, the *Mona Lisa,* is among the most famous in the world. Leonardo was an amazing student who had a great teacher. Later, when Leonardo became famous, he remembered his teacher's help and took on students of his own.

Many great music composers were also great teachers. **Wolfgang Amadeus Mozart** (1756–1791) and **Ludwig van Beethoven** (1770–1827) were very talented, even as children. They became great composers. They also became teachers to help other aspiring musicians.

Margaret Hamilton (1902–1985) is a name you may not recognize. You probably know her better as the Wicked Witch of the West from the movie *The Wizard of Oz.* Before Hamilton was an actress, she was a kindergarten teacher. How would you like to have the Wicked Witch of the West as your teacher, my pretties?

Mrs. Frank had more textbooks to pass out.

"Math is going to be very important for us this year, too," she told the class. "We use math for calculating and measuring in every aspect of our lives—from grocery shopping to building houses and making clothes!"

Carlee liked that a lot. There were a ton of things math could help her do that had nothing to do with teaching. She could be a fashion designer or an architect.

Or a banker!

Galileo (1564–1642) was an Italian mathematician, astronomer, and physicist. He is called the Father of Modern Science. Galileo fought for the idea that the Earth revolved around the Sun at a time when people still thought the Sun and planets revolved around the Earth. Before he became known as a scientist, Galileo taught music. Today, we know that understanding music helps us understand science because both are based on mathematical principles.

Alexander Hamilton (ca. 1755–1804) was a Founding Father of the United States and the United States' financial system. As the first Secretary of the Treasury, he helped establish the U.S. Mint, which produces the nation's coins and paper money—including the ten-dollar bill, with Alexander Hamilton's face on it.

Albert Einstein (1879–1955) is one of the most famous scientists of the 20th century. He was also a great mathematician. His famous equations and theories about energy and matter led to the discovery of atomic energy. Einstein came to America to teach because he knew the United States offered people the freedom to think and do as they pleased.

After lunch, it was time for language and literature.

"We are going to learn about great writers and famous speakers this year. We are going to write short stories and poems. Most of all, I hope we can all increase our enjoyment of reading," said Mrs. Frank.

Carlee loved to read. She had already read a bunch of books, even some of poetry. *If I am good at reading and writing, I can be almost anything, like a book author or a reporter or an English teacher. Wait! Not a teacher! Maybe a lawyer. They get to read and write a lot!*

In the mid-1800s, the **Grimm brothers** in Germany collected, wrote, and published folklore. Some stories were fun, but some were very frightening to young children because they included witches, goblins, and lots of evil, gruesome people. Still, many of the works are just as popular today as they were back then. They include Cinderella, Hansel and Gretel, Snow White, and Rumpelstiltskin. Besides being great storytellers, both of the Grimm brothers held teaching posts at the University of Berlin.

Charles Lutwidge Dodgson (1832–1898) is better known by his pen name Lewis Carroll. Carroll, was a great English writer, mathematician, photographer, and teacher at Christ Church, Oxford University. Kids know him best for his books, which include *Alice's Adventures in Wonderland* and its sequel, *Through the Looking-Glass.*

Sir James Matthew Barrie (1860–1937) was a Scottish writer and dramatist. He wrote many plays, but can you guess what he is most famous for writing? Here's a hint. Barrie had some neighbors, the Davies family, who had five sons. To amuse the boys, Barrie made up stories about the youngest brother, Peter, who in the stories could fly. Now can you guess Barrie's most famous work? After becoming famous for the novel *Peter Pan,* J. M. Barrie was appointed the Rector, or principal, of the University of St. Andrews.

The last lesson of the day was science. Mrs. Frank made sure all the children had notebooks to use for their science journals. She talked about all the experiments they were going to do this year and how they would write about them in their notebooks. They were even going to raise crayfish! Crayfish were like tiny lobsters.

Carlee wrote her name inside her new journal and wrote "Science" on the cover in cursive letters. She was excited about all the neat things she would do in science class.

That still won't change my mind about being a teacher. I can do a ton of different jobs with science—I could be an inventor, a chemist, or…

a veterinarian!

 **Louis Pasteur** (1822–1895) was a French chemist, microbiologist, and teacher who created the first vaccines. You know them today as the "shots" you get at the doctor's office that keep you from getting sick. Pasteur also developed a way to preserve food. The process is known as pasteurization. His discoveries have saved thousands of lives.

 **Alexander Graham Bell** (1847–1922) is known for inventing the first telephone and for being a great teacher. Bell taught other teachers at the Horace Mann School for the Deaf. His hearing and speech experiments led him to be awarded the first U.S. patent for the telephone in 1876. Ironically, Bell considered the telephone a noisy interruption into his scientific work. He refused to have one in his study!

 **Marie Curie** (1867–1934) was a woman of firsts. She was the first woman to win a Nobel Prize and the only woman to win one twice! Her first prize was in physics and her second was in chemistry. She was the first woman in Europe to earn a doctorate degree. She was also the first female professor at the Paris University, La Sorbonne.

As the end of the school day approached, the hands on the clock seemed to hardly move at all.

The clock must be broken, thought Carlee. She could not wait for the day to be over, even though she was beginning to think that it really hadn't been so bad after all. She had not seen her mother once, not even at lunchtime.

Just then the clock struck half past two, and the school bell rang.

Carlee walked out of the classroom and saw Ava coming down the hall. All the worry came back to her again.

This is going to be a disaster. Ava will probably snub me. Carlee tried to walk away fast.

But Ava walked faster. "Hey, Carlee, wait up! Did you know your mom is my teacher? She's really cool. I think she is going to be the best teacher I have ever had."

Carlee froze in surprise.

"Really?" Carlee asked. "Are you making fun of me?"

"No!" said Ava. "The whole class thinks your mom is awesome. She is super nice, too. She let us paint with watercolors and let us have popcorn while she read us a story out loud."

Trevor walked by. "Hey, Carlee! Your mom is my new teacher."

Carlee grimaced.

"She is great. Too bad YOU can't be in our class. She let us do a science experiment on our very first day. I want to be a cool teacher like your mom when I grow up."

Carlee's mouth opened, but she couldn't think of anything to say.

Just then Todd walked over. Carlee had known him since preschool. He was always the class clown.

"Carlee, did you know your mom is my teacher this year?" he asked. "I remember when she made us lunch all the time when we were little, but I didn't know she was a teacher. That is way cool."

Carlee's head was spinning.

It stopped spinning only when Ava asked, "So are you going to be a teacher when you grow up, too?"

Todd said, "That would be awesome."

Carlee said, "Maybe."

Carlee said good-bye to her friends and walked down the hall to meet her mother at the front of the school.

Carlee wondered about all the jobs she had thought of doing instead. Listening to Mrs. Frank had made her think about all of them. Maybe that's what teachers really did after all—get kids thinking about all the neat things they could do when they grew up. Maybe doing that wasn't so bad after all.

Mom greeted Carlee. "So, Carlee, how was your school day?"

"Good," said Carlee. "But not what I expected."

Mom smiled.

"So, how was teaching?" asked Carlee.

"I'm happy to be teaching again," said Mom. "It makes me feel good. I like the kids in my class. I hope they come to like me, too."

"I'm pretty sure they already do," said Carlee. All of a sudden she felt embarrassed. *I really should have known all along how cool a teacher my mom would be,* she thought.

"Can I go home with you?" asked Carlee.

"Of course," said Mom.

When they got in the car, Mom said, "Well, I'm glad to hear that you liked your class! Did you learn anything new on your first day back?"

Carlee paused for a long time.

"Well?" Mom prodded.

Carlee took a deep breath and smiled. "I learned I want to be a teacher when I grow up…but maybe not in the same school as my kids."

Photo credits

p. 15. Painting: Charles M. Russell, *Captain William Clark Meeting with the Indians of the Northwest*, courtesy of the Sid Richardson Museum, Fort Worth, Texas.

p. 17. Apollo 11, courtesy of NASA Archives.

p. 19. Photo: Martin Luther King, Jr., courtesy of Department of Defense Imagery, American Forces Information Service.

p. 23. Portrait of Ben Franklin by David Martin, courtesy of the United States White House Collection.

p. 31. Photo: Margaret Hamilton. (Source: Wikipedia Commons.)

p. 35. Photo: Albert Einstein, 1921, by Ferdinand Schmutzer. (Source: Wikimedia.)

p. 43. Portrait of Louis Pasteur by A. Edelfeldt, 1885. (Source: Wikimedia.)

www.ingramcontent.com/pod-product-compliance
Lightning Source LLC
Chambersburg PA
CBHW040017050426
42451CB00002B/11